Animals at the Water's Edge

ANIMALS

at the
WATER'S EDGE

RAINTREE PUBLISHERS
Milwaukee

This book has been reviewed
for accuracy by
Dr. Charles P. Milne, Jr.
Visiting Assistant Professor
Department of Biology
Marquette University, Milwaukee, Wisconsin

Library of Congress Number: 87-20687

  2 3 4 5 6 7 8 9 0   93 92 91 90 89

Printed and bound in the United States of America.

Library of Congress Cataloging in Publication Data

Animals at the water's edge.

   Adaptation of: Animaux du bord de mer/
Bernadette Bornancin, Gisèle Puig.
   Includes index.
   Summary: Discusses fish, seabirds, lobsters and
crabs, seahorses, and other interesting forms of
animal life that make their homes in or near the sea.
   1. Seashore biology—Juvenile literature.
2. Marine fauna—Juvenile literature. [1. Seashore
biology. 2. Marine animals] I. Bornancin,
Bernadette.   Animaux du bord de mar.   II. Raintree
Publishers.
QL122.2.A54 1987   591.909'46   87-20687
ISBN 0-8172-3115-3 (lib. bdg.)

CONTENTS

THE GREAT CORMORANT

A LOOKOUT

Imagine riding in a boat along the Atlantic coast of North America or Europe. Off to one side, you see a large, web-footed black bird, perched on a buoy. Its wings are open, but its straight body does not move. Suddenly, this bird dives into the water. Skillfully, it swims as it searches for food. You have just seen the great, or common, cormorant, a bird closely related to the pelican.

Although its plumage, or feathers, appears black, the cormorant is really a dark greenish bronze. Its cheeks and throat, however, are ivory white. A small triangle of yellowish bare skin outlines the eye showing brightly against its dark feathers. The long neck, forms an "S" shape. It ends in a strong, hooked beak. The short legs and huge, webbed feet make the cormorant seem clumsy as it walks. Yet, these same features make it an excellent swimmer.

EGG-LAYING

The great cormorant nests on the ledges of huge, rocky cliffs or on steep little islands. During the mating season in March, the male and female build a large nest with dried seaweed, twigs, and branches. The female usually lays four bluish or pale green eggs. Both male and female sit on the eggs. They hatch in about a month.

The young cormorants are born blind and without feathers. The parents feed them for about seven weeks.

Then the young take flight. They return, however, to feed on fish that their parents still provide for them. When summer begins, the young birds leave the nest for good. At the age of three or four years, the young birds will have their own young, and the same pattern continues.

UNDERWATER FISHING

Because the cormorant is an excellent swimmer, it is also skillful at catching its food underwater. First, it studies the water's surface. When it sees a sand dab, a sand eel, or a fish, it will dive into the water. It may dive to a depth of seventy feet or more, depending on the kind, or species, of cormorant it is. These dives can take as little as ten seconds. They can also last as long as one full minute. In any case, the cormorant totally disappears into the water.

After it has caught a fish, the cormorant swims to the surface of the water, carrying its catch. It then tosses the fish into the air and swallows it headfirst. The bird will later regurgitate fish bones and other undigestible parts in a red mucous sac.

Even though it is a heavy bird, the cormorant can run on the water's surface. As it takes flight, it begins to beat its wings with strong, powerful move-

The cormorant catches fish in its beak. It throws them up in the air and swallows them headfirst.

ments. It skims along the waves while gaining speed. Finally, the bird begins to soar into the air with its head raised and its wings bent at an angle. Once in the air, the cormorant can fly as fast as thirty miles an hour.

A STRANGE POSTURE

After cormorants have eaten their fill, they perch on a rocky ledge, a tree, or a buoy. They are often found perching in a group. In fact, cormorants may nest in colonies of over a thousand birds! On their perches, they sit very still, with their wings open to the breeze and the sun. It is a beautiful sight. Many photographs have been taken of them while they are in this position.

As with most marine birds, the great cormorant is a protected species. It is a victim of many predators, or animals that kill other animals for food. Often, cormorants get caught in fishing nets, causing them to drown. Nevertheless, there are many cormorants along the coasts, and it is easy to observe them.

There are over thirty species of cormorants throughout the world. The Japanese have tamed one of the species. They use its swimming and diving skills for commercial fishing. These cormorants are tied by a line to the front of a barge. A ring is fastened around each of the birds' necks so that they cannot swallow the fish they catch. The birds are then thrown into the water. The cormorants catch fish and bring them back to their owners.

Because it is a heavy bird, the cormorant must forcefully beat its wings to gain momentum and fly off.

THE VELVET CRAB

A HAIRY CRAB WITH TEN LEGS

At the fish market, you may sometimes see a small, purplish brown crab known as the velvet swimming crab. You can recognize this crab by its shell, which is lined with blue stripes, or by its head with its two dark red eyes. And, of course, you will notice the velvety hairs that cover its body. These give the animal its name.

The velvet crab is a crustacean. Crustaceans are animals whose bodies are protected by hard shells. Lobsters, shrimp and crayfish are all crustaceans, too. In many parts of the world, people eat various crustaceans, including velvet crabs and other types of crabs. In fact, people who like seafood say that the velvet crab is very tasty. But as with all shellfish, you must have the pa-tience to shell it. When cooked, the velvet crab turns a brick red color.

The velvet crab has five pairs of legs. Because of this, it is classified among the decapod crustaceans. The word "decapod" comes from the Greek words *deca*, meaning ten, and *podos*, meaning foot. The velvet crab uses its two rear legs for swimming. They are flat like paddles and are used as oars. But not all crabs move about only by swimming. Green crabs, for example, move by walking sideways. They are able to walk this way with amazing speed.

PREDATOR AND SCAVENGER

Some crabs live deep in the ocean. Others, like the velvet crab, live close to the coasts in the shallow waters.

There, the velvet crab nests in long, brown seaweed that is shaped like ribbons. It is there where its eggs and microscopic larvae, called zoea, develop. As you can see from the picture in this section, each of the zoea has large eyes and a spine that stretches from its back.

The velvet crab sometimes leaves its shelter to find food. It feeds on small live animals that it finds in tidal pools, or in areas along the coast that are uncovered at low tide and covered at high tide. It also eats dead or decaying material. Because of that, it is called a scavenger.

SHEDDING ITS SHELL

Like all crustaceans, the velvet crab is protected by a very hard shell. This is called an exoskeleton. The shell does not grow as the crab grows. So from time to time, crabs and other crustaceans must shed their old shells. When they do, a new one has grown in beneath it. This process is called molting. The velvet crab will shed its shell about twenty times during its normal three-year life span.

The molting process can easily be observed in an animal kept in a marine aquarium. During the period of shedding, the crab's behavior changes. It stops eating, it becomes less aggres-

From time to time, the velvet crab molts and leaves its shell. It only needs a few days to grow another.

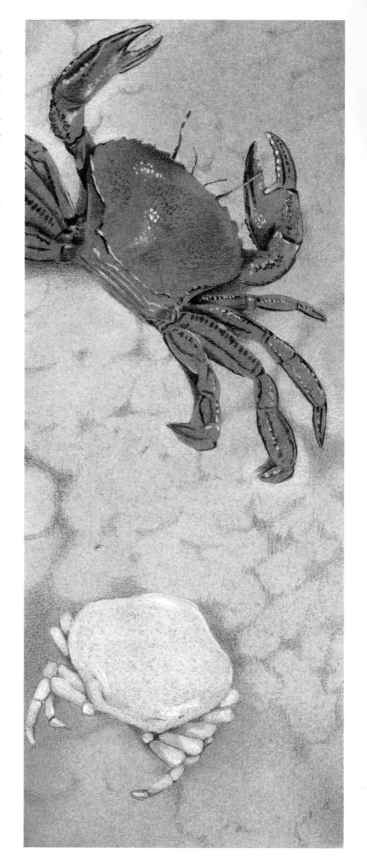

sive, and it hides itself. To break out of its tight shell, the crab breathes in water. This causes the crab to swell and its shell to crack. The crab escapes by wriggling out backwards.

The entire process takes about fifteen minutes. After that, the crab is completely weak and unprotected. It then hides for a few days until its new shell hardens. During this time, the crab is easy prey for crabs, shrimp and other predators. However, within a few days, the velvet crab's new shell has become as solid as the old one. It then continues its normal activities until the next shedding. Crabs captured during this shell-changing period are especially valuable. They are sold as soft-shelled crabs and are considered a delicacy.

A FIERCE DEFENSE

When it senses danger, the velvet crab will usually flee. But if it feels threatened, it may use its first pair of legs to defend itself. The first legs are the crab's claws, or pincers. The shape and size of a crab's claws depends on its species and its habits. But most crabs will use their pincers for defense. You must be careful when picking up a crab. It will twist itself in every direction, trying to pinch you.

In their young, or larval, stages, crustaceans sometimes take on curious shapes.

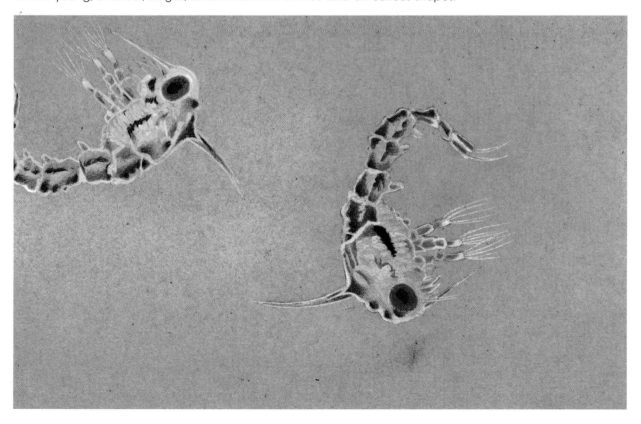

THE PLAICE

A BOTTOM FISH

You are walking along a sandy beach at low tide. You spot a shallow channel of water a few yards away and decide to wade in it. The water is cool and refreshing. It feels as if the sand is moving away under your feet. Suddenly, you see a small cloud of sand disappearing quickly. You have probably walked over a plaice, without even seeing it. It isn't easy to see this unusual creature because it is skillful at hiding itself.

A DISAPPEARING ACT

Plaice is another name for a number of European flounders, or flatfish. The one pictured here is commonly found in the coastal waters of Europe. There are about 500 different kinds of floun-der worldwide. They live in the bays and along the shores of most seas.

The plaice is a grayish brown fish. Its back is sprinkled with red or orange spots. Special cells under the fish's skin can change the size and shape of these spots. In this way, the plaice can blend in with its surroundings, helping it to hide from predators.

This protective coloring is not the plaice's only means of hiding. Sometimes, when lying on the sandy sea bottom, the fish can bury itself. First, it quickly moves its fins to create a cloud of sand. The settling sand covers the plaice. Only its eyes stand out, watching for food sources or possible danger. If the fish spots prey or needs to escape, it can shake itself free and quickly swim away.

A DANGEROUS TIME

It is estimated that the female plaice lays 50,000-400,000 eggs at one time. Each egg is surrounded by food and is enclosed in a little sac called the vitellus. When the egg hatches, the larva is nourished by the food in the sac. This is the larva's only food source until it is able to feed itself. At this stage in its life, it is easy prey for other animals. Many plaice larvae are eaten by bigger fish and small marine animals. In fact, only two or three larvae out of 100,000 survive the first few weeks of life.

FROM LARVA TO FLATFISH

The plaice, like most flatfish, is not born flat. When it is first hatched, it looks like any other kind of fish. But after it has grown about a half an inch long, the fish's body slowly flattens. The young plaice begins to swim on its side. Gradually, its face begins to shift. In the plaice, the left eye moves towards the right side of its head. Eventually, both eyes appear very close together on one side. Not all flounders' eyes shift to the right side of their bodies. It depends on the species. Meanwhile, the mouth and all the bones in the fish's head twist. As you can see in the picture, this makes the plaice look as if it is frowning.

The plaice larva changes slowly as it grows. The body flattens out, and one eye moves to the opposite side of its head.

As these major changes are taking place in its body, the plaice slowly settles to the sea floor. It rests on its left, eyeless side, which turns a milky white. Its upper side becomes darker. The plaice's fins form a fringe all around its body.

LIFE AS A FLATFISH

The young plaice spends this adjustment period near the coast. Later it will join the older fish on the sandy floor in deeper waters. After its first year, the plaice grows more slowly. A full grown plaice rarely gets larger than sixteen inches in length.

The plaice feeds on worms and on shellfish such as mollusks, mussels, clams. With its new coloring, the plaice is able to catch its food much more easily. If its prey is small enough, the plaice will swallow it whole. Larger prey is crushed in the plaice's teeth.

FISHING FOR PLAICE

The plaice and its relatives are popular game fish. But many commercial fishermen also fish for these flatfish because they are an important food source. Some of them, such as the halibut, turbot and sole, may be familiar to you. The species common to North America can be found in both the Atlantic and Pacific oceans.

It is difficult to find a plaice when it is buried in the sand.

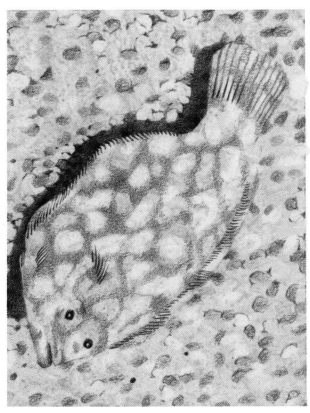
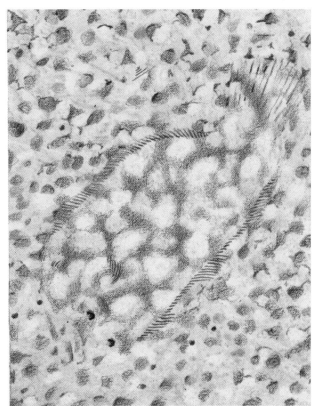

THE PUFFIN

CLOWN OF THE SEA

The puffin is one of the most interesting animals to watch. This colorful bird seems to bounce as it moves from rock to rock. It is a curious and playful creature that will peck at anything that interests it! Its actions have given it several nicknames. "Parrot of the sea" and "clown of the sea" are the best known.

The puffin's black and white plumage is much like that of its cousin, the penguin. Its walk is also similar. The puffin uses its short, webbed feet to move in an upright position. Its small, waddling steps give it an awkward appearance.

During the summer mating season, the puffin's body undergoes colorful changes. Its legs and feet turn a bright red-orange, and a red ring develops around each eye. The beak, which is large, narrow and triangular, develops vertical stripes of red, blue, and yellow. After mating season, the puffin sheds the outer surface of its beak. The beak is then smaller and not as colorful. It will remain that way until the next mating season.

AN UNDERGROUND NEST

The puffin is one of those rare birds that nests in a burrow. It hollows out its nesting place by using its beak as a pick-axe and its webbed feet as shovels. Sometimes it will use last year's burrow or occupy one that a rabbit made! The tunnel may be as long as eight feet.

In the nest, the female puffin lays a

single, gray-white egg. Both parents take turns sitting on it. After the egg hatches, they faithfully feed the chick for the next six weeks.

This is not an easy job. A five-week-old puffin can eat six small fish in ten seconds. The adult puffins are often seen returning from the open sea with as many as thirty small fish in their bills at once. Scientists have not yet figured out how the puffin catches fish while holding other fish in its beak.

A BIRD OF THE OPEN SEA

Seeing puffins is a rare treat. The most common species is called the At-lantic puffin. It lives on the coasts and islands of the Atlantic Ocean. When sailing near the Atlantic coast, you may be lucky enough to get near a group of these sociable birds. They may be floating along on the waves in search of food. If you startle them, they will run along the surface of the water and take flight rapidly. With their short wings, they don't fly very high or very well. But they are excellent swimmers when they dive.

In North America, puffins can be seen only at certain times of the year. Puffins pass near the coast only during the mating season from April to July. The rest of the year is spent at sea far

Several times a day, the adult puffins gather fish for their young.

Puffins nest in tunnels they have hollowed out or in burrows borrowed from rabbits.

from the shore.

Towards the middle of July, the puffins leave the coastal areas and head back to the open sea. Any young puffins are left to provide for themselves. A puffin chick waits days and days for food which never comes. Finally, it leaves the nest and goes to the water's edge. At nightfall, half-flying and half-walking, the young bird flings itself into the water. It then begins to feed itself. It must learn to take care of itself quickly. Seagulls are eager to swoop down on these defenseless birds.

IN GRAVE DANGER

About thirty years ago, there were many puffins along the Atlantic and Pacific coasts. Several thousands of these birds would gather there each spring during the nesting season.

However, a disaster known as the "black tides" has cut the puffin population along these coasts. "Black tides" were caused by oil tankers spilling large amounts of oil into the ocean. Black pools of oil were left floating on the ocean's surface. Puffins and many other birds were caught in the oil. They died by the thousands.

Some ornithologists, or people who study birds, have started breeding colonies for the puffins. Through their watchful eyes, the puffin may not become another endangered species.

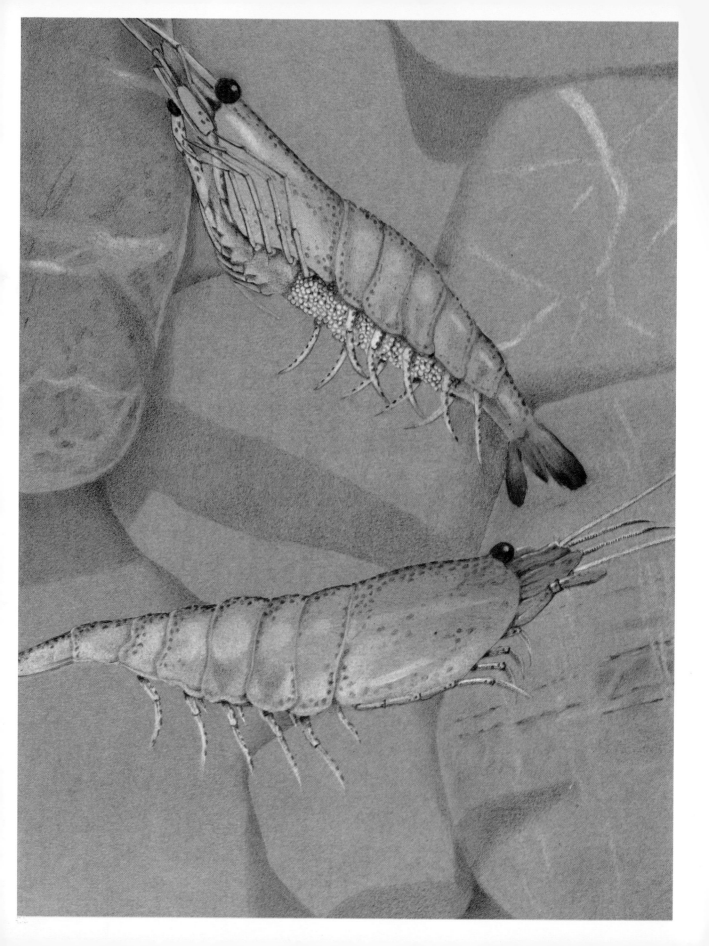

THE GRAY SHRIMP

A FRESHWATER AND SALTWATER ANIMAL

The shrimp is a small shellfish related to crabs, lobsters and crayfish. It lives in many parts of the world in both fresh and salt water. Often, shrimp live in large groups in channels or on the sandy sea floor. Others live toward the shore, where they hide in the mud by day and hunt for food at night.

There are many species of shrimp. The smallest measures about an inch long while the largest can reach a foot long. Shrimp are generally a gray color, although some are brightly colored and have stripes. Some shrimp can even change their coloring to match their surroundings. This ability, known as protective coloration, helps the shrimp hide from its enemies.

AN INTERESTING CREATURE

All species, or kinds, of shrimp have the same general body structure. They have long, narrow bodies and five pairs of legs. The first pair of legs is often a set of claws with which the shrimp eats and fights. The others are used for walking and swimming. The shrimp usually swims forward at a slow pace. When disturbed, it can leap backwards with powerful strokes of its tail. The shrimp's tail is fan-shaped and is the largest part of its body.

The shrimp's head has two very noticeable features: its eyes and its antennae (or feelers). The eyes are two dark spots that stand out from the head on stems. They move in all directions, giving the shrimp all-around vision. The shrimp's two pair of antennae are sometimes as long as the rest of its body. They are used to smell and to touch. They are always moving and help the shrimp find food.

Like its relatives, the shrimp is a crustacean. This means it has a hard shell covering its soft body. This shell, called an exoskeleton, protects the shrimp from harm. During its lifetime, a shrimp will molt (shed its shell) several times. Crustaceans must molt be-cause their shells do not grow as they do. With each molt, the old shell cracks and falls off, allowing its new, larger shell to harden.

THE SHRIMPING NET

To catch shrimp, you must use a shrimp net. As you can see in the picture, this net is made up of three parts. A net with small mesh is attached to a strip of curved wood. This is used to scrape a sandy beach or a channel bottom. The strip of wood is attached vertically to a pole. The fisherman uses this pole to push the net. The wooden strip of the net stirs up the water as it slides across the sand. This disturbs

It is best to fish for gray shrimp at low tide.

A traditional way of shrimping in Belgium.

the shrimp, and they get caught in the net.

SHRIMP FISHING

Shrimp are a very popular food throughout the world. For that reason, shrimp fishing has become an important industry. Commercial fishermen fish much the same as you would with a small net, but their nets, called trawls, are much larger. They are designed to hold fully grown shrimp and to allow the smaller shrimp to escape. This cone-shaped net consists of an opening, called the neck, which scrapes the sand. The upper part is fitted with corks to keep the net open. The rear of the net narrows in order to form a small pocket that is closed by a knot. The trawls are dragged over the sea bottom.

Several interesting methods are used to catch shrimp in different parts of the world. In Wales and Great Britain, a tractor is used to pull the shrimping nets. In Belgium, shrimp fishing is done from horseback. At a slow, steady pace, the horse pulls the net along the water's edge. When the net is full, the fisherman takes the horse to shore and sorts the catch. Only the largest shrimp are kept. They are stored in two wicker baskets attached to the saddle. This traditional shrimp fishing is more than five centuries old.

THE SEA HORSE

The birth of sea horses.

A HORSE OF A DIFFERENT COLOR

The sea horse is a small, unusual fish. It can be found in the shallow waters along seacoasts, especially in the warmer, more tropical waters. This fish is called a sea horse because its head looks like that of a tiny horse. It is also known by its scientific name, Hippocampus. This name comes from Greek words meaning horse and sea monster.

The sea horse is very different from most fish in several ways. For one thing, the sea horse's shape is very unusual. Its stocky body usually grows no more than six inches long and has a long, coiled tail. The sea horse uses its prehensile tail to cling to the eel-grass in which it lives.

The sea horse's large head has a long snout and bulging eyes. The snout is actually a long tube which ends in a tiny, toothless mouth. The sea horse feeds on small water animals which it sucks through this tube. The sea horse's eyes protrude, or stick out from its head and can move separately. This allows the sea horse to see in all directions. It can even look up and down at the same time. Without moving its head, the fish can quickly spot passing prey. This makes the sea horse an excellent hunter.

AN ARMORED ANIMAL

The sea horse is also different than other fish in that it is not covered with scales. Instead it is covered with a kind of shell. This shell is made of armor-like bony plates that protect the fish. The brown-green color of its shell also helps the sea horse. With this coloring, the animal blends well with its eel-grass home. The sea horse's shell is also very hard to digest. This discourages many predators.

A MARINE HORSE

The sea horse does not swim horizontally as many fish do. Instead, it swims in an upright, or erect, position, quickly moving its dorsal (back) fin. It may move this fin as many as thirty-five times per second. Luckily, if this fin is damaged, the sea horse can regenerate (or regrow) it right away. The sea horse swims weakly, using its head as a rudder. Often, it is helped along by the currents.

AN UNUSUAL BIRTH

The behavior of this strange little fish is even more unusual during the mating season. Sea horses mate in the spring and summer. When trying to attract a female, the male sea horse begins to dance. The female soon joins him, and the two fish, face to face, twist their tails together. The male

At birth, little sea horses are left to themselves and must face the dangers of the sea alone.

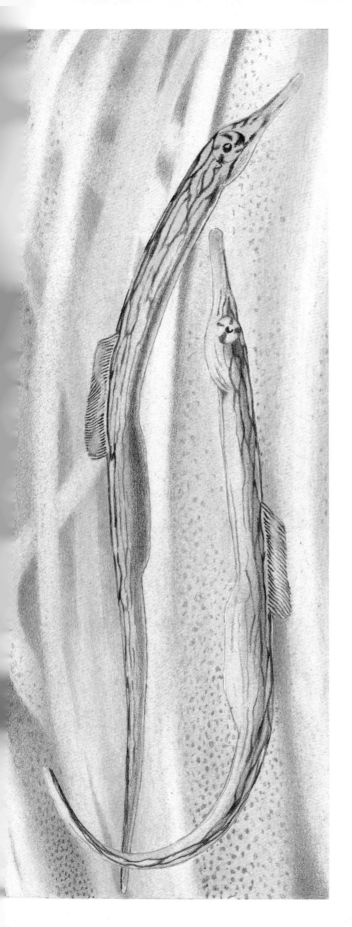

then offers a pouch on the underside of his stomach to the female. The female lays about 200 eggs in it. The male incubates the eggs in his swollen belly. They hatch in about four or five weeks.

It is the male sea horse, then, that "gives birth." By twisting and writhing its body, the male pushes its young out, one by one. It pauses to rest after each birth. A young sea horse is a tiny threadlike copy of the adult. Its head and fin seem much too large for the rest of its body. From the time they leave the pouch, the young ones must take care of themselves. These strange births have often been observed and filmed in aquariums.

The sea horse is a sensitive fish. It does not live very well in captivity. To survive, it must live in an environment that provides running sea water.

A COUSIN TO THE SEA HORSE

The pipefish is a close relative to the sea horse. This fish can sometimes be found in small tidal pools or near coral reefs.

Like the sea horse, the pipefish has a long snout. Its body is also covered with similar bony plates. But the pipefish has a longer, much thinner body. Its nicknames include "sea viper," "sea eel," and even "sea serpent." Despite these names, the pipefish does not bite or sting.

At the water's edge, the pipefish, which is not as scarce as the sea horse, is easy to observe.

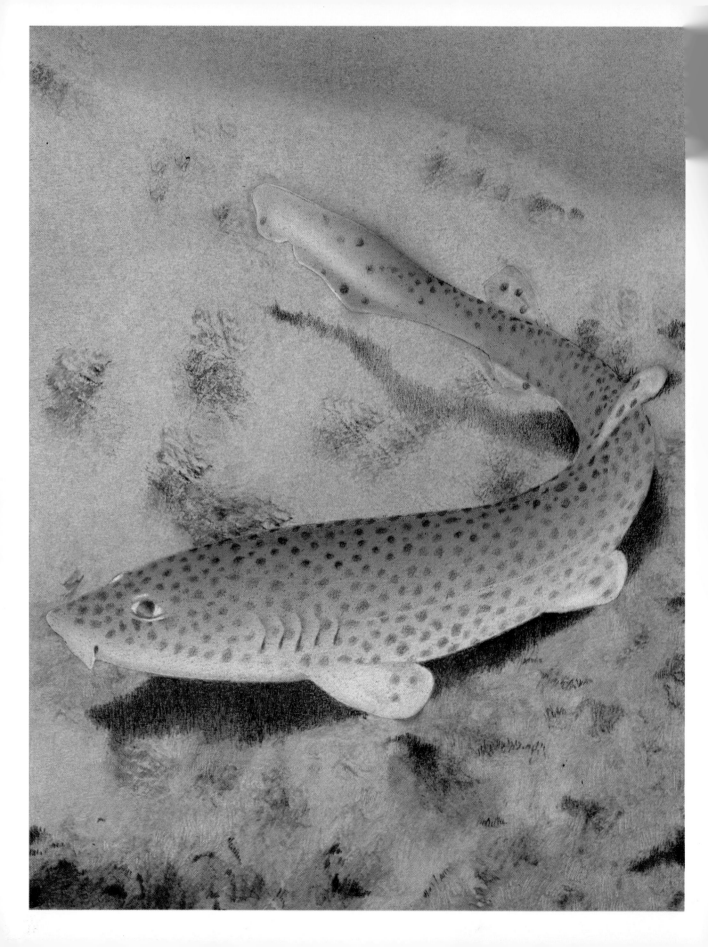

THE DOGFISH

A SMALL SHARK

When people think of sharks, they often overlook the dogfish. Although the dogfish has the general shape of a shark, and the same large, split mouth on the underside of its head, it just does not match people's idea of a shark. Still, the dogfish is a shark. But maybe because of its small size and slightly different shape, the dogfish is often forgotten. After all, the dogfish rarely grows more than three feet long. This cannot compare with the whale shark, which can grow up to sixty feet long.

In general, dogfish are small, torpedo-shaped fish. The dogfish pictured here is the smaller spotted dogfish of the Mediterranean and Atlantic coasts of Europe. They do not have the famil-iar pointed snout of a shark, but they do have the well-known dorsal (or back) fin. Like most sharks, the dogfish has no bones. Its skeleton is made of a tough, flexible substance called cartilage. It also has a pinkish brown skin which is usually flecked with brown or black. The skin is covered with tiny, tooth-like scales known as placoid scales. They make the dogfish's skin very rough. In fact, dogfish skin can be dried and used as sandpaper.

Dogfish are often found in the warmer seas. There they live in large groups along the sandy sea floor in both shallow and deep water. The dogfish is most active at night when it hunts among the rocks for food. There it feeds mainly on crustaceans, fish, and some mollusks.

WELL-PROTECTED EGGS

Between March and September, the dogfish lays about ten eggs. All members of the dogfish family lay their eggs in special egg-cases, or capsules. Each brown capsule is about 2½ inches long and contains one egg. Most species' cases also have long tendrils, or feelers, at both ends.

When they are first laid, the capsules are carried along with the currents. Eventually, using the tendrils, they are fastened to seaweed. In the seaweed, the eggs are hidden from predators. The eggs remain in the weeds for eighteen to twenty-two months. Sometimes, high tides throw the capsules up on the shore. When this happens, the dogfish often do not survive.

FISHING FOR DOGFISH

Dogfish are caught with the help of special fishing lines that are several yards long. Hooks are attached about every six feet and baited with mackerel or sand-eels. Sinkers are used to add weight to the lines. Each line is marked by a floating buoy. These lines are submerged to the sea floor and pulled up several hours later. An electric hoist is used to bring the lines back up. Several

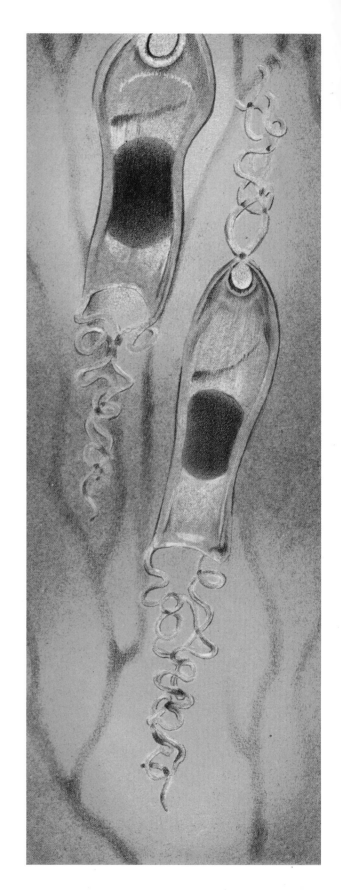

Each dogfish egg is protected by a capsule. This capsule drifts along in the current, and, finally, clings to seaweed.

miles of fishing line are put into the sea every day.

THE AUCTION

When the boat returns to port, the fisherman's work is not yet finished. The fish must still be sold at a fish auction.

The fish are separated according to species and size and placed in containers. The auctioneer then announces the starting price of each container. The fish merchants, who buy the fish and transport them to markets, place their bids. The prices go up or down, depending on the quality of the fish and the market demand.

THE IMPORTANT DOGFISH

In many places, dogfish and other types of shark are considered an important food. But not everyone cares for the taste of dogfish. It is more popular in Europe and Asia than in America.

At one time, dogfish were important for another reason. Fisheries along the Pacific coast of North America once caught large numbers of them for their liver oil. Until the 1940s, the dogfish's oil was a main source of vitamin A. But before long scientists discovered an inexpensive way to make this vitamin without the dogfish oil. Today, few North American fishermen make a living fishing for dogfish or other sharks.

The fish auction takes place early in the morning in a hall. The fish merchants have their warehouses there, and the fish is delivered to markets by truck or train.

THE MUSSEL

A PUMP FOR FEEDING

The mussel is one of the most commonly found shellfish in European and Asian fish markets. Unlike other seafood, this shellfish is actively cultivated or grown. Freshwater mussels, sometimes called clams, live in streams and lakes, while sea mussels live in the oceans.

The mussel is a bivalve. Its hinged shell consists of two parts, or valves. The mussel's soft body is protected by the two valves. They are black or navy blue on the outside and pearly white on the inside. The mussel attaches itself to a rock, breakwater, or other surface with a very solid thread called a byssus. This anchors the mussel, and it usually holds the shellfish in one place. When the mussel is under water, the two valves of the shell stay open and show its orange body. The constant movement of millions of small hairs, called cilia, creates a current through the mussel. Micro-organisms in the water are steered toward the mouth and are then filtered and digested by the mussel. The mussel acts like a pump as it filters up to nineteen gallons of water a day.

CLINGING FOR SURVIVAL

In spring, the male and female mussels produce special reproductive cells. These join with each other in the water to form an egg. The egg develops, changes into a larva which again changes and makes its own byssus. This is a dangerous stage in the life of the mussel. Either the mussel succeeds

Harvesting mussels has become an important food industry.

in attaching itself to something and lives, or it fails and becomes an easy prey for fish.

When you climb along rocks at the beach, you may walk over colonies of wild mussels that have been uncovered by the low tide. Even the smallest of them have edges that can wound and cut bare feet. Mussels also cling to buoys, under wharfs, and at the foot of lighthouses.

If you find a mussel on the beach with its shell partly open, watch what happens when you try to insert a stick between its two valves. It will use its muscles to close itself up tightly. It then becomes impossible to open the shell with your bare hands. The mussel

protects itself in this way when the tide uncovers it. After it is tightly closed, it lives on the oxygen in the water it has stored up. Then it simply waits for the tide to return.

A SHELL THAT GROWS

In summer, the temperature of the water rises and micro-organisms multiply. As it filters out a large number of them and absorbs them, the mussel grows bigger. This growth makes the shell grow larger, and another layer of growth is added to the outside of the shell. In winter when the supply of micro-organisms decreases, the mussel does not grow.

RAISING MUSSELS

Even prehistoric man living at the water's edge made use of the natural deposits of mussels. Mounds of empty shells have been found near ancient dwelling places. Later, the Greeks and the Romans also ate these shellfish. It was in the seventeenth century that mussels were first raised, or cultivated, by people. The mussels were placed on oak posts that were driven into the sand. Later, people harvested the mussels. These days, the raising of mussels has become an important industry.

Generally, mussels are cultivated in mussel beds, on wooden poles which are uncovered at low tide. The young mussels — or spats — attach themselves to cords wound around the posts. They may be harvested after a year and preserved in fish tanks.

A POSSIBLE DANGER

In summer, especially near polluted ports and channels, you should not gather mussels. Because they eat waste, they may become toxic or poisonous. But mussels that are bred are under strict control. The bags in which they are sold are even marked with a ticket that guarantees that they are not a health threat to customers.

Mussels can cling solidly to a surface by means of the byssus, a bundle of silky but strong threads.

THE STARFISH

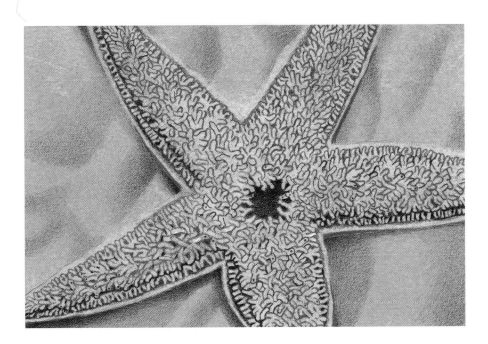

A STAR THAT WALKS

The starfish is a small animal that has arm-like extensions on its body. Sometimes called a sea star, the starfish generally has five arms and resembles a star. The starfish first appeared over 500 million years ago. Today, it can be found in all of the world's oceans. Depending on the species, the starfish may be red, violet, or a greenish yellow.

Different kinds of starfish have different numbers of arms. The starfish's arms make it possible for the animal to move around. On the underside of each, there is a double row of small, movable tubes, called tube feet. Each tube foot has a tiny suction cup at its tip. When the starfish "walks," the suction cups grip the surface of the rocks or sand.

To see how a starfish uses its arms, turn one "on its back" while it is in a pool of water. Slowly, with much twisting, the starfish will flip itself over again. Although the starfish can move, you can see it does not move very fast.

ASTONISHING ARMS

The starfish's arms are one of its most interesting features. In addition to giving the animal movement, they also help it to "see." At the end of each arm is a small colored eyespot. These eyespots sense light. Although they cannot make out images, the eyespots are still helpful to the starfish.

As you can see, the starfish's arms

are very important to its survival. Luckily, like certain other water creatures, the starfish can regenerate, or regrow, arms if the old ones are broken off. Even a starfish that is cut in two can regenerate itself. In this case, each half will grow into a new animal.

STRANDS OF EGGS

Starfish lay eggs into the sea through small openings between their arms. Some species of starfish lay eggs in long, sheer, rubbery chains of light yellow and orange. The eggs are carried along by the tide, and soon form into tiny swimming larvae. These eventually settle down to the bottom of the sea and become starfish.

STARFISH BY THE HUNDREDS

There are many species of starfish. The most common, found on Atlantic coasts, is called an "asteridian oyster." It lives near rocky coasts and even in some ports. The arms of this bumpy starfish give it the look of a perfect pentagon, or five-sided figure. Varying from green to pink, it measures just under three inches long. The starfish can be seen at low tide, sticking to the rocks. There it shields itself from the heat and the risk of drying out.

A MEAL OF SHELLFISH

Starfish feed mainly on shelled ani-

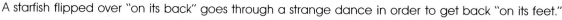
A starfish flipped over "on its back" goes through a strange dance in order to get back "on its feet."

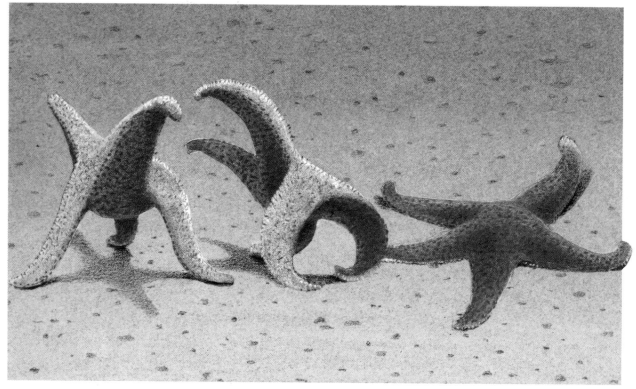

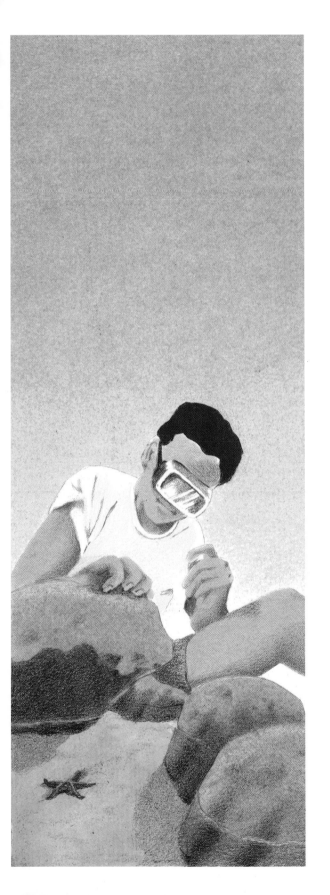

mals such as mussels, clams and oysters. Because of its slow speed, the starfish has a limited menu. It can only prey on animals that move slower than it does or those that do not move at all.

When it feeds on one of these, the starfish uses an unusual method. First it prys open the animal's shell by presing its arms against the two halves, called valves. When it has opened the shell just a crack, the starfish injects a fluid into it. This fluid relaxes the muscles that hold the two parts of the shell together.

Next, the starfish inserts its esophagus and stomach between the valves. A starfish can slide its stomach through a crack only as wide as one thickness of cardboard. It then surrounds the animal with its stomach and begins to absorb it. This is a very slow process. It may take a starfish two hours of constant effort to open a shell. It may then take up to eight hours to eat it and up to twenty hours to digest it.

A DANGER TO SHELLFISH

Because starfish eat large numbers of shellfish, they are a source of worry to shellfish farmers. Starfish can do much damage to oyster beds. Some fishermen are quick to blame starfish for the disappearance of scallops, an important commercial fishing product. They think that starfish should be harvested to slow down their reproduction.

At low tide, the starfish sometimes is a prisoner of tidal pools.

THE HERRING GULL

A LONG-FLIGHT BIRD

The herring gull, a type of sea gull, is a common marine bird. It is found near the seacoasts of North America, Asia, and western Europe. Since it constantly searches for food, you might also see one near inland rivers and lakes.

The herring gull is sometimes called a silver gull because of its light grayish blue coat. The tips of its long wings are black and white. Its stomach, tail, and collar are paler, and its webbed feet are pink. The yellow hooked beak, streaked with red, is strong enough to crack open shellfish.

The gull's flight is powerful and graceful. With its wide, strong wings, it catches the air currents, gliding along cliffs, over ports, or behind boats.

Gulls have been known to follow ships for hours at a time. They seem to fly with little effort and without tiring.

THE FLEDGLING

Between mid-April and mid-May, the female usually lays three eggs. Its simply built nest is lined with grass, twigs, seaweed, and feathers. The nest of the herring gull can be found near rocks or on the ground. Both parents take turns sitting on the eggs for about a month.

When the chicks hatch, they are covered with a soft, fluffy, light brown down. They are fed by both parents. To get their food, the chicks tap the red spot on their parents' beaks. You may be able to observe this feeding process from a distance. When feeding the chicks, a parent bird throws up, or regurgitates, food into the nest. This food, which comes from the parent bird's stomach, is partially digested. This makes it easier for the chicks to eat.

In addition to feeding the chicks, the adults must also protect them. The little gulls' down helps to hide them in the nest. But the parents try to keep predators from even getting near the nest. When an enemy does get too close, the watchful adult gulls immediately attack. Screaming and swooping low over the predator's head, they try to drive it away.

Within a few weeks, the chick's feathers are flecked with gray and brown, and its beak is black. Two months after its birth, the young bird, called a fledgling, joins the adult gulls. But it will be three or four years before the young gull takes on its adult coloring.

During the nesting season, the gulls gather on a cliff or steeply-sloped island. These groups are called colonies. Where their nests are not disturbed, the gulls' colonies may contain several thousand birds. Gulls are known to be loud, active birds. As you can then imagine, a large colony can be a very noisy place.

Sometimes, when gathered together, gulls copy each other by sitting with all their beaks facing the same direction. People who live at the seashore say this

The gull's chicks develop quickly. They leave the nest after a few weeks.

signals that a storm is coming from that direction.

EASY TO OBSERVE

Because of its large size and its fondness for living near people, the gull is an easy bird to observe. When doing so, you might see this long-flight bird swoop inland to drop a clam or snail onto rocks, paved highways, or other flat surfaces. Many gulls have cleverly learned to crack shells in this way.

Gulls can also be seen inland near newly plowed fields. There they feast on worms and other insects that have been turned up by the plow. Because they are scavengers, gulls will often be seen around harbors, near public garbage dumps, and in picnic areas. There they eat fish, rotten meat, vegetable matter, and even the eggs and young of other birds.

TOO MANY GULLS

Gulls have survived because they are able to adjust to different living conditions. Because the gull eats just about anything, it has a constant supply of food. Also, it has no natural predators. This explains the large number of gulls throughout the world.

Because of their large numbers, the herring gulls are sometimes a menace to other marine birds. They steal their eggs, kill their chicks, and chase them from their nesting sites.

Gulls feed at dumps, where they find a great deal of food.

FACTS AT A GLANCE

Scientific classification is a method of identifying and organizing all living things. Using this method, scientists place plants and animals in groups according to similar characteristics. Characteristics are traits or qualities that make one organism different from another.

There are seven major breakdowns, or groups, to this method of classification. They include: kingdom, phylum, class, order, family, genus, and species. The kingdom is the largest group. It contains the most kinds of animals or plants. For example, all animals belong to the animal kingdom, Animalia. The species is the smallest of the groupings. Members of a species are alike in many ways. They are also different from all other living things in one or more ways.

THE GREAT CORMORANT

Phylum:	**Chordata** (vertebrates)
Class:	**Aves** (birds)
Order:	**Pelecaniformes** (water birds with four webbed toes)
Size:	32 inches long
Reproduction:	4 eggs per year
Habitat:	Seacoasts throughout the world, especially those of North America and Europe
Diet:	Fish

THE VELVET CRAB

Phylum:	**Arthropoda** (joint-footed animals)
Class:	**Crustacea** (hard-shelled)
Order:	**Decapoda** (having 10 legs)
Size:	Up to 2½ inches long
Reproduction:	20,000 to 25,000 eggs are laid in seaweed beds
Habitat:	Rocky, shallow coastal waters
Diet:	Waste, small dead animals, water plants

THE PLAICE

Phylum:	**Chordata** (vertebrates)
Class:	**Osteichthyes** (bony fishes)
Order:	**Pleuronectiformes**
Size:	Up to 16 inches long
Reproduction:	50,000 to 400,000 eggs at a time
Habitat:	Sandy or muddy bottom areas along European coasts
Diet:	Mollusks, small crustaceans

THE PUFFIN

Phylum:	**Chordata** (vertebrates)
Class:	**Aves** (birds)
Order:	**Charadriiformes** (shorebirds, water-feeders)
Size:	12 inches long; wingspan of 24 inches
Reproduction:	1 egg per year
Habitat:	Arctic waters of Atlantic and Pacific oceans
Diet:	Fish, small crustaceans, mollusks.

THE GRAY SHRIMP

Phylum:	**Arthropoda** (joint-footed animals)
Class:	**Crustacea** (hard-shelled)
Order:	**Decapoda** (having ten legs)
Size:	8 inches long
Reproduction:	200 to 300 eggs laid in deep water.
Habitat:	Sandy coasts and channels, in both fresh water and salt water throughout the world.
Diet:	Plankton (small drifting plant and animal life)

THE SEA HORSE

Phylum:	**Chordata** (vertebrates)
Class:	**Osteichthyes** (bony fishes)
Order:	**Gasterosteiformes**
Size:	6 inches long
Reproduction:	Female lays about 200 eggs in male's pouch
Habitat:	Seaweed fields along more tropical seacoasts
Diet:	Small fish

THE DOGFISH

Phylum:	**Chordata** (vertebrates)
Class:	**Chondrichthyes** (cartilage skeleton fishes)
Order:	**Selachii**
Size:	48 inches long
Reproduction:	10 eggs per mating season. Eggs are laid in special egg-cases
Habitat:	Rocky or sandy sea floors in warmer regions
Diet:	Crustaceans, fish, mollusks

THE MUSSEL

Phylum:	**Mollusca** (soft-bodied, enclosed in a shell)
Class:	**Bivalvia** (bivalves)
Order:	**Mytiloida**
Size:	3 to 6 inches long
Reproduction:	Numerous eggs are deposited into water
Habitat:	Freshwater mussels live in streams and lakes; sea mussels live in oceans
Diet:	Micro-organisms taken from water

THE STARFISH

Phylum:	**Echinodermata** (spiny-skinned sea animals)
Class:	**Asteroidea**
Order:	**Paxillosida, Spinulosida, Forcipulatida**
Size:	8 inches in diameter
Reproduction:	Releases numerous eggs into water through holes between arms
Habitat:	Warmer waters of all oceans
Diet:	Mollusks, sea urchins, bodies of small marine animals

THE HERRING GULL

Phylum:	**Chordata** (vertebrates)
Class:	**Aves** (birds)
Order:	**Charadriiformes** (shore-birds, water-feeders)
Size:	22 to 24 inches long
Reproduction:	3 eggs per year
Habitat:	Seacoasts of North America, Asia and western Europe
Diet:	Fish, crustaceans, eggs, food scraps

GLOSSARY/INDEX

Bivalves   animals, such as clams or mussels, that have two hinged shells. (p. 35)

Byssus   a strong thread or string with which mussels anchor themselves to rocks. (p. 32)

Crustacean   a large class of animals whose bodies are covered with hard, shell-like coverings called exoskeletons. Lobsters, shrimp and crabs are all crustaceans. (pp. 11, 23, 32)

Dorsal fin   a fin found near or on an animal's back that helps it stay upright. (pp. 28, 31)

Exoskeleton   the hard, shell-like body covering such as that of the crustacean group. (pp. 12, 24)

Mating season   specific times of the year in which animals come together to breed. (pp. 19, 28)

Molt   to shed hair, feathers, shells or other outer layers. (pp. 12, 24)

Plumage   the feathers of a bird. (pp. 7, 19)

Protective coloration   a means of defense in which an animal's coloring helps it blend in with its surroundings so that it cannot easily be discovered by its enemies. (pp. 15, 23)

Regenerate   to grow a new body limb to replace one that has been lost. Crabs, for example, are able to regenerate claws and legs. (pp. 28, 40)

Regurgitate   to throw up partially digested food. Some birds feed their young by regurgitation. (pp. 8, 44)

Tendril   a slender, coiled, and sensitive organ used to attach an organism to its support. (p. 32)